Phantom Limbs

poems by

Deirdre Fagan

Finishing Line Press
Georgetown, Kentucky

Phantom Limbs

Always, always for my children

"Keep Fighting"

for yourselves, for each other, for all of us

With love
for the family I created, the one I fought to keep,
the families I chose, & the ones who chose me

Copyright © 2023 by Deirdre Fagan
ISBN 979-8-88838-367-4 First Edition
All rights reserved under International and Pan-American Copyright Conventions. No part of this book may be reproduced in any manner whatsoever without written permission from the publisher, except in the case of brief quotations embodied in critical articles and reviews.

Publisher: Leah Huete de Maines
Editor: Christen Kincaid
Cover Art: Shelley Stevens
Author Photo: Jennifer Johnson
Cover Design: Elizabeth Maines McCleavy

Order online: www.finishinglinepress.com
also available on amazon.com

Author inquiries and mail orders:
Finishing Line Press
P. O. Box 1626
Georgetown, Kentucky 40324
U. S. A.

Table of Contents

I.
Phantom Limbs 1

II.
it must be strange to be a house 5
Times Square, 1977 6
Driven Thru 7
Spring 8
Sleepover 9
A Kiss 10
The Unnamed War 11
The year Frank Serpico attended my Halloween party 12
The kindness of strangers 14
Knowledge 15

III.
Father's Botany Lessons 19
Rose Colored Lovers 20
Upon a Poem 21
And then you can't breathe 22
Kith 23
The Last Unveiling 24
Twice Believing and Twice Knowing 25
Have Love 26
No One Knew 27
It's All Over Now 30
Superstitions 31

IV.
Notre Amour, Comme une Pomme, Vient de la Terre 35
X, Y, C 36

The trouble with pairs 38

To the person in charge of discontinuation: 39

While your husband is still able to stand 40

The Last Time Making Love 41

The Month of the Dead 42

In Memoriam 43

V.

All the previous deaths were un-posted; word came by
  ring tone or Post, not post. 47

Anointing the Dead 48

Call me Charon 49

Remember this: 50

Going Hungry 51

Most of the Days of the Week 52

River Among the Gravel 53

When you reach to flush the toilet and your hand looks
  exactly like your mother's 55

The Height of Gladness 57

Homesick 58

VI.

Spilling forth 61

When a leaf blowing in the wind seems like a hello. 62

Kinder Garden 63

How Contentment Comes 64

Love Begets Love 65

Stepping Up 67

Bartering in Michigan 68

The Widow Remarries 69

Doorbell Advised 71

Outside In 73

Gardening is an honor system 74

Melding Metal with Metal 75

The Widow Gets a New Mattress 76

Everything I hate about you, I love about you, Dear 77

Between Us 78

Knotted We 79

VII.

The Dancer 83

Realizing I should have never peeled a mango—
the skin is delicious 84

Secret Sauce 85

Night Giblets 87

Dish by Dish 88

What it is Now 89

Love at Assisted Living 90

The thing is. 92

When I am, play me recordings of those I loved, while I'm— 94

i couldn't throw you against a wall 95

Abandonment 96

Ordinary Sounds 97

At the Opera House 98

VIII.

A Birthday Poem for Us 101

I.

Phantom Limbs

I tell my son each family has a tree.
I pencil lines on a page leading to his father, his sister, me:
"People, like trees, have branches."

Branches in our tree bow abruptly on one side:
One cracked unceremoniously—it was brittle—
Two committed suicide—snapping off willfully—
Another was in slow decay and was whittled away…
in each, the bark exposed the core.

I know, but do not tell.

I also recall, slowly, with lead, how else it is done:
other boughs break, peeling, cracking, succumbing—
only one splintered edge at a time.

On one side of my hand-drawn sketch,
the angled and slanted lines extend only toward absence—
one generation back, and the whole already begins to recede,
inching ringless, limbless, toward a well-known cliff.

Completing the halved tree, I tell both of my children, as I gesture in their direction:
"All families have trees—this one is yours—."

II.

it must be strange to be a house

feet on your floorboards,
individuals dusting your windowsill.
the chimney drawing deeply
your often-held empty breaths.

when i was a child, i dreamt of climbing
over doors and around light fixtures,
the house upside down, or me.
they say a house is not a home,

but once you can feel the switches,
navigate light and dark, you are
where you are, whether you want
to be or not. it must be strange.

to be a house is to be always
inhabited by others, a container
for those who invade without notice.
knocks at the door often unwelcome.

when i was a child, i crept across the ceiling,
safe from whomever was below. safe keeping
was in my own hands as i swung legs over
doorframes, escaping myself room by room.

Times Square, 1977

I put the quarter in and turn the crank,
my first images of pubic tufts,
round bottoms,
silent film.

Adjacent to my eight-year-old body:
A fully rounded, bosomy blonde hips her cigarette,
glistening, as my teenaged brother, emerald-eyed
acquiesces.

Mounds of green plastic bags far rounder than her bottom
mount the cracked pavement in droves,
the stench winding soda-sticky in the direction of her pelvis.

Babysat by a slice, a dog, and an egg cream, I wander the arcade,
scanning the floor for abandoned quarters.

Years later, the island scratched clean by Giuliani and radiating light,
I'm reminded of the rhythms of those nights.

Unsupervised,
I inhaled the epicenter of Manhattan—
Maclaren strollers and diamond-studded Daisies absent—
smacking my bubble gum and cracking my knuckles,
waiting for my brother to heel out his hand-
rolled smoke in the gutter.

Driven Thru

When you are 13 and poor,
even Taco Bell has an allure.

The Monte Carlo that held us
had a sheepskin bench seat.

Its soft cover like a fitted sheet
curving its corners like a cloud.

Seatbelts weren't worn in 1983;
no need for slits to let safety peer in.

"Come closer and you can steer," you said.

Nearly half my current size, no breasts,
thighs the width of my current calves—

I leaned full-bodied into the drive
eyes on the road, mouth watering,
drive-thru beckoning.

(What is there to taking a young girl?)

Spring

Cow-speckled hills
full-bosomed bushes
these are the things of spring

Monolithic magnolias
blossoms pivoting
release their loveliness

Grassless mounds
suddenly burst forth
emboldened seeds

Lovers tilt heads toward lips
as eager as mid-summer sunflowers
lean toward the sky

Peering deeply into new eyes
the brush with breath brings
a surprise flick of the tongue

Fall will be sudden when it comes

Sleepover

a plaid pullout worn down down down
springs poking deep my tiny back
a blanket slowly uplifted

cool air shocking warm slim-thin thighs
stomachpelvisclenched muscles tight
large hands and cotton underwear

the panties pulled quietly aside
lips first felt hot wet pointed tongue
thick fingers slowly entered then

i tried to control my breathing
and pretend i was still sleeping
in the next room your wife asleep

the next morning i dare not say
mother sent me over to stay
fourteen—first sleepover away

A Kiss

A kiss can be pithy
And concise—
Brevity the soul of it.

It can cause the jaw to ache
With the momentum of
A lucid tongue.

It can ride the surface
Like a whimsical dragonfly
On a pond.

It can be a waterslide
Of uncontrolled saliva, a
Bloodhound's drool.

It can meet head on
Like a train thrusting into
A station.

But yours is an anchor
Plunging depths, full throttle,
All of the mystery gone.

The Unnamed War

I had come to a darkened apartment in Jordache jeans—
only a teen. In the five years spent, I grew breasts, grew up,
but couldn't leave, not yet. I had been drafted and there was
a war in that house; I had not yet known how to cross the line,
how to leave the country already mapped for me.

By flying to a foreign land—my father's house—I escaped that
not home the summer the Arizona sweltering scorched all records.
I was twenty years old and had traded my only possession of value,
a fourteen-year-old Buick, on a street corner to an immigrant
who handed me his life in a money order.

I shipped what little I owned in tattered boxes & landed on
father's doorstep, scars intact and weary from the journey,
but afraid to tell its horrors. Sixteen candles had been blown out
by you, one by one. But some fire was still burning, enough to
drive the body back east where it belonged.

I, in safety, now sat on the second story of father's duplex
having escaped war in that Arizona desert just before the radio
announced the U.S. was going to war in the Persian Gulf.
Surrounded by flowered wallpaper, in lamplight, I shuddered,
remaining in fear of the flight of survival I had well come to know.

The year Frank Serpico attended my Halloween party

We carved Jack-o-Lanterns
while the two Franks talked.

My father, Frank,
a retired leader of NY Dems.
You, a retired cop known for a love of animals—
and for ratting out the rats in the NYPD.

When you met my dad,
you probably had a mouse in your pocket,
you often did.

My father raised me to care about the underdog.
He once told me, "Rooting for the Yankees is
like rooting for US Steel," and his most
recounted day from his years spent
drafted into the Army—
the morning after JFK.

Dad's reveille on November 23, 1963:
"The President was shot—
by a White Southerner!"
He was stationed in Korea &
speaking to a group of "racist
Southern boys," he said.

After the pumpkins had been carved,
we lit candles and dimmed the lights,
lined them up on their death row,
the kitchen counter, and stood,
in a row, opposite, judging.

One was characteristically clever,
another grimaced,
several were large,
and the round one, the one on the end,
quite small, the simplest of all:

two triangle eyes, a round nose,
and a smiling mouth.

In the quiet dark, Frank S. broke the silence:
"That one on the end is the scariest of them all."

The kindness of strangers

When I think of the tenderness of airplane travel
I almost cry

Seated in rows, often six across, among strangers

there is so much courtesy in the passing of a cup
civility in abandoning a seat so another can relieve himself

There is beauty in the everyday action of not reclining a seat

In the handling of another's trash

And then there is this. This other thing.
There.
On the news.

And we cannot close our eyes to sleep among the strangers
and we cannot close our eyes

and yet we still do

We sleep soundly 10,000 feet in the air

Knowledge

Mostly we are unaware
of ourselves

We fumble familiarly
our minds navigating their spaces
our bodies rounding corners
absently avoiding debris

Upon extending an arm
at the right height
of a doorknob
while staring ahead
without blinking

we enter our bedrooms
where we are suddenly surprised
by the faint recognition
of our own
scents

III.

Father's Botany Lessons

"Purple loosestrife," you said as you drove.

The opera blared on the public radio station
while I sat consumed in thought.

I recalled your having pointed that out
the day before, on our way for ice cream.

"It chokes out everything around it," you said.
"Huh," I said.

We spent hours that summer driving to town for
household goods, food, odds and ends.

"Purple loosestrife," you'd regularly announce with everything
from recognition to a bellow to a hushed whisper.

"It chokes everything around it out," you'd say, pointing,
the repetition of your line becoming a chorus of country curves.

You tried to talk me out of it, "you don't have to do this,"
you whispered in my ear as you walked me down the aisle that June.

It was the summer of lessons in botany,
or relationships, perhaps.

I still wonder which as I educate the children I chose to have
about the weed.

"It chokes out everything around it," I inform them, remembering its
radiant color and yours, and wondering what I mean, what you meant.

Rose Colored Lovers

I eyed what I thought was a tomato
on a rose bush and reflected,
which is more succulent?

One makes lovers, the other sates,
but which nourishes?

I would like to live on roses, each petal's dew cascading over my tongue
as guileless as a cherry tomato's—the skin punctured tenderly,
the penetration barely delectable.

Upon a Poem

You
make
love
to the
poem
with your
voice,
deep
throating
your
vowels,
stroking
your
T's,
Body
und-
u-
lating,
neck hair
e-
rect,
You
sing
your
O.

And then you can't breathe

The mortgage is too high
The job suffocates
Your cat puts fur balls on your tongue

The food won't go down
The dog lies on top of you
Children, playing, grip your throat and won't let go

Cinch your belt, they say
But the marriage is already too tight

Kith

When you drive by a car with a
woman screaming, windows up,
and the man in the passenger seat—
scarcely visible through the glazed glass—
gives you a furtive glance.

The Last Unveiling

For Matthew (1971-2020)

Apartment to apartment, dorm to dorm,
Across the country by plane, I carried you.

You were a soft and silky "little number,"
Plucked from the shelves, or was that me?

From shopping mall to honkytonk hotel room,
Later donned to make others feel special, not you.

Knowledge changes how we see an object, how we see
Ourselves—no longer as objects to be donned or to adorn.

Gauzy, lacey white panties, matching camisole,
I held you in my hands, seized by your sudden presence.

Alone, in a modest single room apartment, me unpacking,
Soon-to-be husband out of sight and sound,

I saw you for the first time, even though I'd worn you
For the one who laid out on the bed and urged: "Twirl."

He 31, I 13, ages inverted, I now 26, I curled your apparition into a ball
as the sheer fire of you cleaved my mind.

We split ourselves in two. She before.
She now.

But you, Love, saw from the other room, draped your robe over my clothed,
soon-chilled figure, and walked me gently into the night.

An empty darkened lot, a dumpster, me, and a match lit,
then a tender touch from your hand as the fire and power became mine.

The wooden stick, so small, I flung to the gravel, myself still numb.
As the flames quickly and quietly consumed that little number,

White innocence turned yellow smoked hot
& I began to slowly remember who I now was.

Twice Believing and Twice Knowing

Sometimes you want to believe a thing into being.
It's the same with some marriages, only the opposite.

People think you get married when you know,
but that's not the way it happens with so many things.

You believe a thing, the way you believe you will die
before thirty, but then sometimes you live, until 80.

You believe it, but then you don't make it, not even to
the first anniversary because believing isn't enough.

There's the science of it, and the tolerance. In science,
we can measure what can be tolerated for how long.

But tolerance—science can't provide an equation for it
that will help to leverage the blows.

Sometimes you can't sustain your belief for even a year,
while some can sustain it till death.

Believing in a thing doesn't bring it into being,
but knowing a thing can make you believe it.

Have Love

We don't have to mate for life to
make love.

And by make, I mean give,
I mean have,
love.

I had love before you.

But in the period of giving love,
we give something to ourselves.

Something like this smoothed,
shiny stone that no longer has
rough edges but can
still
sink.

Some was not love.

No One Knew

I.

No one knew when I met a boy over a bong
on New Year's Eve, months after my mother
died, and before my story reached my lips,
that it was the untelling of childhood
that drove me to him.

A boy without a driver's license,
without I.D., without a checkbook,
into his arms and waterbed I came.

I don't have to tell you
he wasn't the first.

II.

The first engagement happened
on one knee in a restaurant,
but my mother's cancer
grew in the desert, and that boy
was all water, and the sand
knew.

Mother was dying
and the boy of my youth was driving cattle
while the dust devils enveloped my heart,
so he drove me too.

Sometimes it is the past that beckons the firsts to your bed.

Each boy broken off can put a piece of you together.

III.

One engagement, one divorce, two rings in the tree now.

IV.

The second marriage was clever and kind, the first boy
to hear of the untold man of my childhood.

He loved me anyway.

V.

But there is a kind of love that brings more love.

It welcomes in the dark and the light with heart, mind, and arms,
tongues, the eyes seeing each other and oneself reflected at once.

This love is the one that brought forth two beauties,
shining, whole, unharmed, as yet untouched.

Our beloved was taken, but our love still grows.

IV.

Four rings total in the tree; four rings removed from the finger.

One more ring.

V.

The fourth and the fifth rings are the hardest to tell apart.

They are both beautiful.

They share the same stone.

VI.

No one knows the journey.

The untelling of a childhood sometimes dooms us to repeat it,
the first one we tell may not always be the one that sticks,

the best one to stick may not always be undone by the past, and
another marriage is not always a curse. It is often a blessing.

Each marriage scroll rolls and unrolls a newer older you.

VII.

There are others like you who fold origami-like
into the animals they become through the glee
that turns into the hardship that shakes them free.

I've met them. I will tell you.

It's All Over Now

My mother liked to say:
"He used to kiss her on the lips,
but it's all over now."

While young, I was certain I knew
its meaning.

My parents divorced while I danced to
Ella, who sang of other's pastures looking good.

I don't remember my father ever kissing my mother;
nor did they ever wear wedding bands.

A photograph of their wedding day does not exist;
it's possible it never did. It's possible his love for her didn't either.

Later, I discovered how quickly some kisses travel.
They are a gateway:

"He used to kiss her on the lips, but it's all over now."

Mother always smiled when she said it,
but I now know she wore father's infidelity across her hips.

Superstitions

We believe
if we say a thing
we risk it becoming true

like when we say
"I haven't gotten sick yet—
knock on wood."

We do the same with
I love you

IV.

Notre Amour, Comme une Pomme, Vient de la Terre[1]

After Alfred Sisley's, "Nature Morte Aux Pommes"

First I was one. Then I met you.
I leaned in. You buttressed me.
We leaned to—you to me, me to you.

The shape of apples reminds me of you—
semi-prone on the bed, your roundness lifted in the air,
one blushed cheek to the silk pillow, left leg bent and cocked to the side.

Remove the stem and stand my apple top to bottom—
you are upright at the sink, shaving, your lovely backside
to me. You are beauty drawn, round and full.

Hold me in the hollows of our love as long as the blade lies supine.

When the knife inevitably comes to our wholeness and sections,
one slice stands apart and gazes at the aching open, color now absent from
both middles, yet each ripe with the hope of return.

When cleaved, let it be in parts that summon the before time of
one, then two, then we, all laid more open and more complete by that which
began simply with rounded backsides that beckoned.

---

[1] Our love, like an apple, comes from the earth.

X, Y, C

In the dead of night, I reach for your hand beneath mounds of covers,
my breath almost visible in the winter's cold.

I stroke your wedding band, a circle of platinum, securely rubbing its cool metal,
fully aware of the distance between its arrival and now.

A warm southern breeze sweeps over me as I lay my hand over yours
and take in the rhythms of your breath.

Wiggling my toes in remembered sand, I succumb to memory as your inhales
and exhales recall the crashing waves of vows which transported us from surfside
to this inside, here.

An ivory dress, a crisp suit, bare feet, the horizon, lifted chins, the absence of time
or future.

We were thinner then, unweighted by a life which neither of us was even half-
aware had a distance so fleeting no memory would be long enough or deep
enough to narrow.

My ankle reaches for yours. Draping my leg across the inches that separate, I
longingly navigate the covers with my toes,
seeking the warmth and softness of the top of your foot.

My ankle descends, and for a moment, there is contact. Arm still reaching, hand
atop hand, I am part X, part Y as I splay hand and foot, effortlessly longing
to return you to my seaside, if only for a moment.

There is a grumble, an arch, a pivot, a rolling away, a deep sleep exhale.
And then a back.

Abandoned, left upward facing and sprawled, I am jarred from memory
back into winter.

Receding into a C, I am nearly at the beginning again, conserving the warmth of
my own body, receding in my mind to a future when my reach will be unmet
by your warmth, not by a turned back but by the absence of one.

Your ring will be in a memory chest, your soft feet sanded away,
your breath with my memories of waves crashing.
Or, my ring, my feet, my breath.

Aghast at this sudden vision of everlasting winter, I inch my full body in your
direction, seeking the fullest body warmth—belly to back, knee to back of knee,
lips to back of neck—which consoles, if

only
temporarily.

The trouble with pairs

I want to be inside of you
No, not like that

I want to unzip you
And climb inside

Big toe first, then
a dipping of my head

Until I'm fully upright
and enclosed in your dark

Your sinews and synapses
making room for all of me

I don't want to meet
where lips meet, anymore

Or where parts may be
joined, but inevitably part

I want to get inside so far
there is no getting out

Where two truly are one
and departure becomes impossible

Close is never close enough

And isn't that the trouble with
pairs?

To the person in charge of discontinuation:

It began with swathes and hues of reds I loved.
The lipsticks were removed, then the bras.
Before long I knew better than to like something too much.

If the tights fit perfectly, I would return and wander the store casually,
pretending I was looking for something else, and then behave
as though the five added to my cart at the last minute were an afterthought.
I wasn't sure who was looking.

I got in the habit of buying at least three of anything I loved.
Three sweater dresses in different shades; shoes in black and brown.
Be practical. Don't choose the red. Don't lose control.

I knew it was a risk when the husband-father and I only birthed two children;
my own father eyeing the first had said, "You have an awful lot invested,"
but it was a challenge to secure another. She was added to the cart just closing.
Not everything we desire is plentiful.

I was intent on securing enough love.
I didn't yet allow the knowledge of how common warfare is for civilians.
I still believed I could gather enough in my arms to never run out.

An unending supply of nourishment for us all.
Husband-father was not only discontinued but recalled.
And there was only one. Just one.
All the hues of my life reflected in his face.

While your husband is still able to stand

you fasten the tabs
by reaching around from behind,
and your wrist is tickled by his hairy
middle, while you lean in, close your
eyes, and pause to smell the skin on his back.

when your husband tells you to call
what he's been wearing diapers
because that's what they are,
you do.

his head lowers as you finish the job.

When you get groceries, he encourages you to
take your time, enjoy being without him,
not to rush home, he is clean. He will be fine.

no matter how many times you tell
him it doesn't matter to you,
you will be unable to unburden him.

upon learning, as you set down the groceries,
he has called an aid, instead of you,
a gift to you, the way he used to do
the vacuuming, or bring you flowers,
your own head will lower.

you will place the ice-cold coffee you have
brought him beside his chair and thank him
for being alive.

The Last Time Making Love

He is still—unable to move.
The work you used to do together now yours alone to do for you both.
The laundry, the cooking, the shuttling of the children to and fro,
the furniture rearranged, and now your husband lifted by you and moved
where we now must go.

You look into each other's eyes knowing there is little time for such
things in these last bare hours; there is barely enough air to pass through him
to achieve the goal—what you could early on spend a weekend enjoying,
you had to later achieve in quick fixes before the young steps on the stairs
or the sudden tap at the door disrupted all.

But here, now, you grip the bar that helps him move and climb his body
knowing every smooth and bristled surface, you repeat in your mind not to
ever forget his warmth, his scent, or the crevice in the center of his chest
where you found your home. Do not avert your eyes—
know that this has to be forever.

The leverage of the bar becomes part of both of you as you, willing to do
everything for the man you love will these punctuated moments:
be beautiful, be perfect, be the lasting few minutes to an end that makes you
both whole. In the temporary joy that comes, you both experience a release, a
pleasure knowing that this time, at least, time did not matter, and the parting
was satisfactory.

Spent, you lie on his chest, beads of sweat joining in the crevice, and you both
rest in the last after love made with the assistance of a hospital bed equipped
with railings and a bar for leverage. It is the final respite between hospice
visits. After, the children will enter this doorless dining room and return you
to the movements that will remind you your eyes are no longer able to gaze at
the same horizon.

The Month of the Dead

It seems wrong now, but at the time it seemed the most sensible thing
to suggest that October was the month of dying.

You told me you didn't want to make it to the holidays;
you didn't want one like this.

The hospice nurse, standing by the back door, told me you wouldn't make it
to Christmas, told me you were ready.

"He's waiting for you," she said.

After stumbling to the minivan and driving blurry-eyed to pick up the kids,
I came numbly home, knowing the end was near.

The next time we were sharing, I made a tongue-in-cheek remark about how
the other four had all died between August and October, two in October,
so that at least by the Day of the Dead, the mourning season is past.

"Maybe October would be a good time…" I winked, "if you were looking to get
out."

You always did consider what I wanted.

The weekend you died, the sun stopped shining on Friday, and didn't shine again
until you were gone two days later.

Your breaths were so shallow, your voice barely audible, our love for each other
and the children as immense and powerful as the sun that reflected on the leaves
that had yet to fall.

In Memoriam

Sometimes the worst thing that can happen
is the thing that already has

When the worst thing that can happen
does happen, you think, "The decks are cleared,"
but they're not.

There is a worse thing,
always a worse thing.

Rather than anticipate its arrival
or recall the last quake—

Stir, stir the soup.
Light the candle.
Wash your face.

Call your mother, your wife, your daughter, the neighbor.

Call the one or two you've got left.

Then eat.

V.

All the previous deaths were un-posted; word came by ring tone or Post, not post.

The first death by email was Linda's,
the stunned silence of a monitor, your face.

You raced down the hall and leapt,
shrieking to your then-well husband, "Linda is dead!"

You have since committed the crime of alerting,
signaling death's sentinel by a mouse-click of Send.

When your husband died, you kept him home one more night,
the urgency of a funeral home, a coroner, not your own.

You slept on the futon beside the hospital bed in the then bedroom,
once dining room, where you had at one time only celebrated.

The next morning, he no longer resembled the man you had wed.

When the gurney took your Love out the door, you sat before the monitor,
stunned, and alerted all you knew through the only words you had left.

Anointing the Dead

I leaned into her body, just beginning to cool, and brought
my lips to her forehead. I brushed her hair as she once had
mine. I, now, the matriarch of the remaining men.

I had previously brought my mouth to his
closed casket. Brother older by six years;
I hadn't seen him in one.

Other brother, you died lonely, unshaven,
unclean, of too much drink. Red hair greased,
face sallow; not the man I knew.

Father, your forehead already grown cold.
I pressed my lips to your familiar face,
scenting only memory; some can't kiss back.

Love, you parted your lips for me often
during the end, but having lost muscle strength,
could no longer pucker: mouth open, as when learning to kiss.

When we are born, we are covered in kisses,
long before we can kiss back. Later, we kiss for two—
mouths open, ready to receive the anointing with hallowed breath.

Call me Charon

I ferried four out of five of you to Hades

The remaining one traveled alone

3,000 miles away, no one identified his body,

not even the parents

So it goes when you have already been traveling the river Acheron

The second, my mother, took her last breath shortly after I walked out the door

I was a mere mile away, dinner in the microwave after a long day bedside, when I received the call

Her last breath, within thirty minutes of my departure, moments after my stepfather's head had turned to the nurse at the door

Father went in my home while I was growing young minds a few blocks away

Father's heart stopped. He was found with a bite of a ham snack still resting on his tongue

The second to last, also three thousand miles away, took Lethe instead and slept it through. That's the best I could hope for you, brother

My love, number five, you bore the blows of the first two and consoled me through the latter two and then requested me bedside and wide-eyed for your departure You didn't want me to miss it

And before your body was taken, I spent one more night with you

Hades' got nothin' on you

Remember this:

On this Memorial Day, remember my mother,
kicked out of the Army for having sex.

Or was it for being female?

No, not for being female, but for sex,
No, not for sex, but for the result of sex:
my eldest brother.

I can't visit Mom's Army-issued plaque—
it is miles away on a hilltop on the edge of an abyss.

That brother, the first, lies nameless next to her
creating pinecones that litter the ashed bones of each of them
because no such plaque could be issued for a boy, aged 25,
dead, by his own hand, to a mother poor and living on a mountain,
to a father also poor, living on a different mountain, also miles away.

The commander told the father he had better marry that girl,
better make it right
better to not shame the military than to not love the girl.

Two more children and fifteen years later the marriage was still not right,
not made,
not made right.

Fifty-five years later all those good soldiers now dead,
except the daughter, the youngest, me,
the last to be made by the Army-issued family,
the Army-issued not love that begot no peace, only war.

Only she remembers,
only I, only I
remember them all.

Going Hungry

You sacrifice your grief like a meatball,
the last one, to your daughter, four,
who is still hungry—needing more

Most of the Days of the Week

On Monday you make pancakes, pay the bills, clean the floor, wipe down the counters, and begin chopping vegetables for soup. As the knife slices the onion thin, you peel away its outer layer and consider committing seppuku at noon.

On Tuesday you start the Crock-Pot, dust the blinds, rake the leaves, strip the beds, and carry the laundry downstairs. You put the wash on delicate, cold, and as you turn to go upstairs to the hum of the washer balancing its own mind, you longingly consider freshly washed, warmed, and crisp sheets tied gracefully around a rafter and your neck. Those beams appear strong.

Wednesday after tucking the kids into bed and starting the dishwasher, you wash your face, brush and floss your teeth, and line every pill bottle in the medicine cabinet up on the bathroom counter before considering what they will find in the morning. Then you carefully place the bottles back in the cupboard, turn out the lights, and climb into bed yourself, after checking the breaths of your children.

Thursday night you have a little bit too much to drink. Some wine. Several beers. Rum in a hot cup of tea. Then you remember something Nietzsche said about thoughts of suicide getting many through a dark night. This week you've made it three and a half days, but it isn't the weekend yet. You aren't sure if N is right, but you know you can't drink the antifreeze.

Friday you go out for groceries and consider high speed, a curve, a tree, or maybe that bridge over there. But you probably wouldn't even be successful and then what a mess you'd make. No one would be there to clean it up. And the kids. Who would make them breakfast?

Saturday, you roll over to turn off the alarm but there isn't one. A blessing. Shortly thereafter there are kids on top of you, climbing over you, giggling, offering to get you coffee, begging for eggs and bacon, and so you make your way to the kitchen.

When the grease in the bacon pan begins to sizzle, you don't imagine dousing yourself in it or starting a grease fire. Instead, you serve up breakfast and sip your coffee admiring the life you have created, the one still in the making.

River Among the Gravel

The dog is listless and the sky nothing but clouds.
The kettle is on the stove but not boiling.

Yesterday's rain formed a river among the gravel
snaking towards the road. The skylights splashed with lightning.

The last time we saw each other you
were going through airport security.

Your looming body lumbering among those
half a foot below.

You looked like a fish out of water,
a man without a future.

The Eagles said there was a shimmering light
on a dark highway, but it's nearly all pines here

and what's left of the leaves below is
tattered by gypsy moths.

The suet is swinging, waiting for,
or having just said goodbye to

the pileated and oh, how you would laugh,
if you were here.

A bird nearly as big as you,
in birds anyway,

and with a laugh something like yours,
high and bright, but also a bit off,

a recognition, perhaps, that something
was never quite right.

The rain can be torrential, even in the desert,
and the ground covered is more than we ever want to know.

Best to light the flame, listen for the heat, and let go.

When you reach to flush the toilet and your hand looks exactly like your mother's

And suddenly you are twelve,
and she is sitting on the toilet,
and you are standing with your back against the stall door,
and you are watching her change her pad and put in a tampon,
and she is bleeding, and she cannot stop it,
and the government doctors at the county hospital don't stop it.

And you cannot stop it,
because she is dead and has been for twenty-five years,
and the doctors couldn't stop the cancer either,
or maybe they could, if they hadn't sent her home,
and told her to quit smoking and come back the next year.

And so you hug yourself, yourself three years shy of her own last birthday,
and you hold her in your arms, you, all that's left of her,
and you cry in that stall.

And then you remember she had Harvey Wallbanger underpants,
and they fascinated you then, with the recipe on the butt,
and you look down at your ankles and imagine them there,
and you laugh as the tears run down your face.

Your own bleeding was stopped years ago; the insurance you had helped.
And your daughter hasn't even gotten her period yet.
And you wouldn't even be here if your mother hadn't lost your older brother in a bathroom stall, in a toilet, at a movie theater.

A miscarriage that caused that doctor to declare:
"If the next one makes it, if there is another one—
I'd advise against it—
she'll be a girl,
because girls are stronger,
in the womb."

Two boys made it before you—
the first made it nearly half as far as you,
the second made it a little less than ten years shy of her—

the boy whose hands, a little larger than your own,
also looked exactly like hers.

You stand, wombless, a mother, a daughter long motherless,
and flush, your hand wrinkling as it compresses the cold handle,
and greet your own daughter on the other side.

The Height of Gladness

I breathe you in, what's left of you, the oils from your skin still wrinkling these smooth sheets, balled up in a dusty closet, sleeping in the dark.

Your ashes were taken to the dump the day before yesterday (the garbage men don't know).

Your books still line the shelves, the lines you wrote at dawn, singing to yourself.

You hummed off the road and into a dream, the minced meat still on your tongue, while I, opera-soaked, walked myself into a corner and got hung up on a rack. The peace plant died two weeks ago, the one brought by Lucifer and his side-kick Jezebel, its last blossom a burnt sliver of a pod clinging clay-side.

I sit in the corner, imbibing to the last, and imagine you whole.

When I go, ashes to ashes, front to back, closed in on myself like a folded sheet of paper, spread me out, iron me, crease me, but no hospital corners, no, not for me.

Roll me in crackers so that the birds believe they are dining at the Ritz, then shove me off a precipice at the height of gladness.

Homesick

Sometimes you are homesick,
and your puppy,
presumably feeling badly for you,
brings you a dead and gutted rabbit,
as a gift.

"But I didn't get you anything."

I washed the blood from its paws,
disbelieving someone so young,
was capable of such harm,
such dismemberment—
a kind of love.

And then all the violence blazed—
the tearing, the images, the tears,
and disbelief was no longer what I felt.
I felt memory; I felt harm;
I felt dismemberment.

I lie gutted, but still feeling love
for you all.

VI.

Spilling forth

Do you ever feel like the ideas are
        spilling out of you,
                pouring out of you,
like if you could do it over
and over
and over
you might be an architect
        and create walls
or a plumber
        and drain sewage
or maybe you would race
        not on tracks going in circles but far, far away?

But instead you close your eyes and drink in the sounds of babies
        and of love

              You recall the tingling sensations of lips, the scents of the unknown,
and you know it's for the love of the thing, not for how far it takes you away from, or
              closer to
        yourself, but how far you can stretch   without breaking
that matters
        that becomes a sort of profession,
              I mean
confession
held

Dear,

When a leaf blowing in the wind seems like a hello.

I smoke my cigarette in the cold
staring up at a sky littered with stars
and talk to you about the kids, your stocking
hanging on the mantle,
Another holiday come while you've been
gone, another year survived without you.
I know I should be breathing in your scent
instead of the soot and nicotine, I
apologize for being far less than
I hope to be, but remind you that I baked your
favorite cookies, that while my ass is bigger,
my heart is too, it expands and expands,
filled to near-bursting with longing, and
when I exhale the last puff of peace, these
ten minutes visiting you in my mind, alone, here, shivering,
a speck on the planet talking to what specks of you are left, but also to no
one since we both know full well your ashes are ten feet away in the other direction,
through two layers of glass, holding forth in a cabinet, a sudden rustle
of leaves blows my way and I peer down at the driveway and spontaneously blow
out, "hello," and the largest of the group raises its head, or seems to, and waves.
And again, I say hello. And I pretend you hear.

Kinder Garden

When wee, you had squeezed ants to their quick deaths between pink-polished tiny pointer and thumb: "It's because I love them," you had grinning said.

Lifting a rock, you, now three, eagerly asked whether your sitter would also be watching over the squirming pill bugs while father and I were out.

Ladybug umbrellaed and polka-dot skirted, the pink-petaled world was all beneath the magnolia and magnificently yours then.

By three and a half, young father had been terminally diagnosed. Doc McStuffins stethoscoped and fortified, you listened closely, and then inoculated him best you could.

We both felt we had arrived when on one of our last family outings, your small hands easefully clicked on your own seatbelt in the high-backed booster of the white minivan.

By then, we both simply wanted you out of diapers before ailing father would necessarily wear them himself; in the rearview mirror, it was what we could see that we first noticed.

Later, when you tied your own blinking shoes, I alone stood astonished by how far you had come—your dexterity, the knowing tilt of your head, the now sad lilt of your eyes.

Glitter-shoed & sunglassed (even if worn upside down), by four, you had most intrepidly learned of loss and of love and of their most unsubtle differences.

How Contentment Comes

In the quiet of a Sunday morning when with covers over my head the children play quietly while I sleep until ten, I wake completely before joining them, making myself a double espresso bedside before journeying to their needs. Upon making breakfast, a poem surprise discovered in yesterday's pile of mail greets, and reading quietly to myself, my mind awakens to words and to thoughts rising to the unsoiled newness of late sun and of day sounds like bacon and laughter. I have not yet had to do anything in these early moments that I did not want to do, and there was no suffering in any of it. I may be able to ride on these brevities all of my life.

Love Begets Love

The night my mother died,
neither the man I'd recently slept with,
nor the one before who had given me a ring,
answered the phone.

The one who showed at her funeral,
I hadn't dated in four years.
He was happily betrothed to another.

But this time, you,
you were there.

Holding the children's hands,
inciting a pillow fight,
rubbing the small of my back,
holding my sobs close to your chest as I wept.

But that's not the story I want to tell.

I want to write about your curves.

When I first held you,
I couldn't help but compare,
Larger hands, slightly less hair there,
a lot more there, slenderer, quieter.

You, not him.

I compared you,
unfairly, of course, as one does.

But now I have gained a new voice singing,
a new voice singing, whistling, rather
a new life signaling life,
an urging forward.

Love begets love.
Loss begets loss.

But in this moment, now,
your curves,
the supple texture of your back,
your breath warming my cheeks.

Stepping Up

Some people become parents through adoption,
Others, by not wearing a condom.
Some step into it, bringing children of their own.
Some, like you, enter the challenge green,
And partway through the game.
The day I knew you were becoming a father
Wasn't the day you taught our youngest to ride a bike,
Or held our son close for the first time.
It was while we were new,
Their biological father now in a box,
A child now on your lap, at my kitchen table,
When for the first time, without hesitation,
Or a syllable missed in your sentence,
You leaned forward around the girl,
And with one hand slid the full milk glass
12 inches to the side, out of the way of her
Enthusiasms, and, in so doing, awakened mine.

Bartering in Michigan

For Frank Robinson

Sometimes you barter a trombone for a pick-up.
Sometimes it's a fixed vacuum for a six-pack.
We barter in any relationship.

I bartered with you. Two kids. A dog.
One dead husband; two ex-husbands.
You, one ex-wife; a few girlfriends.

When a six-pack is equal to a fixed vacuum,
you are good to go.

The Widow Remarries

I had been wedded before my late husband and I met.
Wedded to an idea, an idea of love.

I was yearning for it, if there's a difference
between wed and married, which perhaps there is.

When we met, my late husband said he worried I fell in love too easily,
as though this would somehow tarnish the love I had for him.

But I looked up for him,
and found him looking admiringly down at me.

He said he wouldn't fall,
but then he did. I had already fallen. So,

I climbed on a rock, water trickling beside,
and turned down my chin, cradling his warm cheeks,
my nose to his head, his head to my chest.

We married, oh so happily.
Deep breath: "I love you."

Years later, I learned that those happily married
are far more likely to marry again, after.

It's documented.

Years later, I held him close,
cradled now in a bed not of our choosing.

It had guardrails in case he should fall.
By then he had become accustomed to all kinds of falling.

Falling in love is dangerous.
It is tricky, but also like riding a bicycle.

Legs supple, go round and round,

in tandem,
until we marry,
again.

Doorbell Advised

In aisle five they sell wireless doorbells with a
150-foot range—battery life 3 years for chime,
2 years for buttons for your new home, in this
old house, so your husband waits while your
legs take you to the world to get one
It had never before occurred to either of you that you would
need one, the old one rang just fine, for the house,
it wasn't until ten years into the marriage that his
muscles began failing, and not long after that the glass bell could
no longer be rung with a twist of his wrist that it was advised
Upon your return, your own wrist deftly
maneuvers with a knife the relentless plastic
packaging, freeing the two buttons and the
receiver you hope will save you both from
fear and further incapacitation
You have a dozen choices for chimes:
foghorn, steam engine, church bell,
the buzzer that sounds on a
game show answer
gone wrong
Last time he cried out for you, you were upstairs,
crying into the phone, you didn't hear him, not at
first, and then you did, and there he was,
down those many stairs and through the kitchen,
straddling the tub, having begun to
fall when he turned from the john, having
caught himself between the legs ten minutes
before, and still unable to get up
You hadn't known. You hadn't heard—
his voice having already grown faint
Now when the foghorn blows, you are assured you will
descend, you will right him when he tips, or falls
between the bed and the wall,
again, you will remain his loving sentinel, you will
cradle what remains of all 200 pounds of him,
folded into you the way he has before folded
all three of you into his chest
Until the day he cannot ring

First the depression of the button asking too much, and then
life itself, and the silenced buttons and this
receiver are put away in his drawer, in the
bedside table on his side of now
only your bed
And once you move to where the children will learn to play
again, one button will be placed in the kitchen, and another
next to your new marriage bed, in an again new home, with a
new husband, and you will ring the children instead,
and they will respond in harmony with gleeful anticipation
Foghorn, steam engine, church bell, the buzzer that sounds on all
game shows gone wrong—and only you will
bear the difference, and shudder from the ignorance of
just how long these new batteries can
last

Outside In

Sometimes I look inside my house and wonder who lives there—

Paintings on the walls, books lining the shelves, a dimly lit chandelier hovering above a single lit candle on the dining room table

Once I pulled into the drive and there was a boy leaning forward to light the candle, a girl setting the table, a man at the sink—a painting exhibiting chiaroscuro

No one else peering in would know this father had just entered the scene, that the girl has nightmares, that the boy has nestled and locked a hidden place that recalls his father's deathbed breaths

What brush strokes captured the scene best, or at all, and what would be revealed should the frame change, should some of the paint be scraped away to reveal the original strokes, and more simply, how the mother about to arrive down center would present?

That evening observing the peaceful scene, the cold outside holding me in place, the warmth inside beckoning, the dog nudged me just as I was entering the stage of hopeful dreaming

Gardening is an honor system

Broccoli goes with tomatoes,
tomatoes like onions,
strawberries remind me of you

You on my hip, your tiny hand extended.

A few dollars placed in a jar.

May. You were barely two.
   You who had come into this world ginger-
   topped, screaming face crimson.

The fruit picked, then bitten, the cap handed back,
a small hand reaching—an exchange of red.
   Again. Again.

Strawberry all over your face and body,
   calyx discarded in a box at my feet
      your father then driving, grinning.

Your hips are now widening, your face pimpling

First Father's ashes dangling from your neck
Second Father kneeling beside you in the garden

Adjusting the wild strawberries climbing unexpectedly
       you dig barehanded in the dirt,
              and make room for new seedlings

Melding Metal with Metal

A brass diamond lies in my palm on the morning of our wooden anniversary,
perfectly cut by you, and holding at least partly the weight of us,
while the early sun shines through the porch window.

Reflected in each of its polished facets, as I roll it about,
wiggling my fingers in a sort of gleeful dance, I recognize
our earlier softer shape now heated, cooled, honed.

Brass is a substitutional alloy: atoms of copper and zinc replace each other
to form the whole—but replacement was never what we were after,
nor what was best.

Head-to-head, peering at its stable, broader top, together,
we find the flat of this brass diamond reflects in its smoothed surface
both, no, each of us.

I attempt to stand the diamond precariously on its fine point,
and am reminded of how we began, singularly, unstable, while
its sharp point pricks at my palm's lifeline.

I turn the diamond on its head, and we, again together,
marvel at how it now spreads outward with confidence,
stability achieved, perfected.

"Wood burns," I say, as we pass from palm to palm
this brass diamond reflecting in its wholeness
five golden years of union.

The Widow Gets a New Mattress

She has been preparing to let go.

A raft in the corn fields of the Midwest after
winding its way north on asphalt rivers.
The interludes and caresses it once afforded,
images now creasing freshly ironed sheets.

It had been the somewhere to which
she had returned, comparing all others
to its quilted arms. He had never slept in it
without her, as later, she must without him.

Babies were made and comforted on its
pillowtop; the mattress first holding two,
then three, then four—two children to
cushion the blow of husband loss.

Then came the wear of more years, the
sink and then the fluff of new life, new love;
the previous one was lifted away—
the new one arrived.

"It's not my old one…." She wistfully tells
friends over wine. From across the room,
the new one, winking at her, says:
"That's what she used to say about me."

Everything I hate about you, I love about you, Dear

The way your coughs fill your pockets.
And you leave crumbs like Hansel.

The way the dog grapples for your attention.
And you shed as you walk.

The patches on your sweater cover holes.
Only I know which are truer.

You bought me the wrong flowers.
And by wrong, I mean the plastic ones.

But I love that these flowers won't ever die,
they'll merely gather dust—and that when you do,
I will not lament your excess in things.

Between Us

My husband takes the dog along
to gather the mail.

His grey matching winter's muzzle,
a retriever seamlessly blending into snow.

The walk to the box is as long as a meadow;
a city block to remember from whence he came.

Once, there was no dog, no country home,
only letters through a slit in the door.

Four bedrooms, one occupied—no children,
no wife.

We are nearly ten years into this game—
we're still playing.

But that's not what he's thinking as I eye
him from the window—the dog flanking his calves.

It's the distance that excites, it's the return;
it's the marrow between us.

Knotted We

After Jason Quigno's Infinite Flow

Hip to ear,
Elbow to lip,
Intertwined &

"She loves me;
She loves me not"

'Round and 'round
Petal by petal we
Daisy ourselves infinite.

"Knot me;
Knot me not"

Breath to clavicle,
Toe to treacle,
Nose to nose.

They say love is—
But ours is blessedly knot.

VII.

The Dancer

Tomorrow I will fall in love again with a dancer nimble on her feet,
and the one appearing in nearly every museum I've entered, with a diva on
stage, and with the one in my living room who calls me by a familiar name.

I will give my heart to the strangers who break records, those who hit
the highest notes, as well as to those who walk when inspired to hit,
known and unknown.

I will give myself, again, to the beauty of the human.

I will also wince as you pass, weighted by a life no one has ever earned,
and ache for the beauty that somehow rides the gusts that leave cigarette wrappers
airborne.

Realizing I should have never peeled a mango—the skin is delicious

I scrape the bottom with the thin blue spatula,
easing every morsel of tomato from the glass rim
into the saucepan. The faucet gifts a few tablespoons
to the jar I now shake, catching the scent still clinging.

As I pour the pink-tinged well water into the pan
and gaze out at our sunned forest, I am reminded
of my own childhood. When in my adult life
had I neglected to daily recall the familiar

moves my mother had made when
our own weekly grocery budget
was no more than $25.00, when her
wage was less than $3.50 an hour?

I had at least momentarily forgotten want,
forgotten need, as I and my children placed
items into a shopping cart trip after trip,
without care for the total.

As the sauce begins to summer, I smile at how
my mother prepared me for battle as I responsively
don my warrior armor once more and remind myself
now is another opportunity to teach my daughter gratitude.

The sauce is bubbling when we have an early
taste of dessert before supper—a novel and welcome luxury.
"Take a bite," I say, and there is delight on her face
as the mango drips down her chin.

Her mouth curls into a smile, the peel at one time
composted, now tingling her tongue.

Secret Sauce

I hadn't become much of a cook yet—
I had only lived, or half-lived, with a few boyfriends,
trying out Shake-n-Bake and pre-packaged jambalaya,
stirring the pot on sofas, kneading love on countertops.

I was home from college, visiting for Christmas,
thinking long term—I wanted to know how to make your
homemade sauce, how you learned to love again after my father
cheated on you and left.

I jotted down ingredients on frayed notebook paper.

As we talked about love and sex, I grabbed my stepfather's
bingo marker and stamped circles all over the pages,
counting my lovers and wondering,
Were my two fathers really the only two men you'd ever slept with?

You died almost 25 years ago,
but I make your sauce and still taste your love
and wonder what you'd tell me now, if you could know.

Four marriages and two children later,
those torn sheets are in my recipe book—
the paper yellowing a little more each year.

I'm still carrying the secrets I could never tell you,
but I've doled them out like recipes to lovers,
a single ingredient at a time.

Last year, risking all, I gave your recipe as holiday gifts.

This year, your granddaughter you never met,
when asked to contribute her favorite recipe to a school cookbook,
picked "Mom's Spaghetti Sauce," believing it mine.

When I wrote the recipe on crisp new paper,
I pictured you—young, tucking a wisp of auburn hair

behind your ear, deftly fingering a cigarette in one hand,
and stirring the pot with the other, and I smiled,

and hoped if I could tell you now, you would no longer let me leave
because I'll never understand why you let me go.

Night Giblets

After boiling, I dice the giblets thin,
then chop, chop, chop.

The dog waits at my feet for a morsel
of love, as we all once did, before we
could see over countertops.

Childhood is a sliver of light before noon, cutting
through clouds sure to carry us into the evening.

I scissor the sage and slide thyme through my fingers,
recalling footed pajamas and mother sounds.

I've been at the top of the food chain some dozen years now,
but I was a child once, licking gravy from spoon on tipped toes.

Liver, heart, gizzard, neck, whole, extended, longing for more, before
afternoon sliced ever so thinly inward and served me savory, au jus.

Blunt knife slides the giblets across the cutting board and into the heat
where the fatty broth waits for night to come and be welcomed by me.

Dish by Dish

Today, I filled the sink with soapy water and carefully removed
all the china from the mahogany cabinet, dish by dish.

Sun reflected in the glass during my final push of the darkened door,
grandmother's egg coddler and the pinecones from your uncle's
grave shifting among the urned ashes, as I wiped my hands
on my worn apron, pondering what sits in any cabinet.

Sometimes, it's all too much.

Scalding my hands, I gently sponged and dried each, then
brusquely stacked them on the everyday shelf above the banana
tree, toaster, and breadcrumbs, among the canning-jar drinking
glasses, and father's cheap floral plates nostalgically glued back together.

Tonight, and every night, we will dine off the Haviland,
occasionally breaking one, or with some hope, two with daily life.
We will will the letting go with laughter, with crashing joy, and
without wincing.

After it all, what are we waiting for?
Or is it *whom*?

What it is Now

Sad isn't what you think it is as you get older.

It's not being called names—
that hardly makes you wince anymore.

It's not crashing on your bicycle and having
the gravel picked from your knee in the ER.

It's a gloomy day, yes, but only when it's the
thirteenth in a row and you miss your mother

who's been dead almost thirty years, but even that
isn't the sad it's come to mean, come to be, is it?

Sad is a grip of awareness that one day your children
will, maybe, miss you, but not like you think. They will sit here

each by this tree on this cold bench and remember the year you shook
to the heavens about the broth, hours spent simmering on the

stove, now all over the refrigerator, stove, floor, the dog, your slippers.
"It isn't going to be Thanksgiving now, is it? Is it?"

It wasn't going to be, but not because of the broth. Because of you.

Love at Assisted Living

They say assisted living is more like
a dormitory than a nursing home.
Those arriving uncoupled, rarely stay so for long.
Those who arrive coupled and lose, often gain again.
The same is true if there is mobility, that is,
the opportunity to get around.

You wandered the halls not knowing what (or for whom)
you were looking, but knowing you needed to find a way
home. You called the closest you could call to
home—a cousin in Minnesota—your birth state—
where you hadn't lived in some fifty years.
but she couldn't assist you.

While she had helped move you in, she didn't know
where you were when you phoned: which hall, which floor,
what memory you were lost inside. But soon you were found,
and the two of you sat side-by-side for months watching TV,
holding hands, solace and calm and ease—home at last.

When Valentine's Day came, we sent chocolate-covered strawberries
and phoned, and I could almost hear the melted chocolate on your lips—
smell the sweet strawberry still left on both of your tongues. Your new love
spoke, thanking me for sending them—for enough for two—maybe, even, for you—

Later, TV blaring, you hid yourself in the bathroom and sat on the lid of the toilet,
whispering into the phone line: "Don't tell anyone, but we rode the bus to
Walmart, and he bought me new bras and panties." "He treats me like a
queen," you gushed over and over and over—you who had to heal your own
before bruises—the strawberries that more than once fist-bloomed along your
collarbone—had been made queen just before memory's final lapse. You never
thought it could happen to you.

Still later, you began to sugarcoat over and over and over the late husband who
had hurt you. You had long since stopped asking about the new love who had
been whisked out your door, back to his own birth state—whose name was
quickly lost on your still upturned strawberry lips—but I'd like to think you went

out a queen in fresh bloomers, surrounded by scents of strawberry and smiling, his name the one ripe on the tip of your tongue.

The thing is…

We are all characters,
characters in a play,
a play of our own making.

And we can change the set,
and the lights,
and the stage.

Wear make-up,
or not.
Hell, even a wig.

We can even alter
our character,
or play several at once.

But the music—
so little of that is in our control.

And the audience,
the one we imagine and prepare for,
rarely arrives.

The one in the front, center,
is the one who came—
not always the one we want.

And when the tickets sell,
it's often not for the right reasons,
whatever they are, but most certainly the wrong,
which we usually know, or can at least imagine most clearly.

The marquee always gets it wrong.
It's salacious, and we are all bones, atoms,
and other things not illuminated by lights.

So the show goes,
sometimes with tap dancing,
and we sing.

When I am, play me recordings of those I loved, while I'm—

I made bread for you as we baked.
Dinners were divine.

We checked our numbers, our temps,
Our coughs as we popped allergy meds.

At night we watched movies when we were spent.
Read when we were in need of escape.

And we considered our odds,
Like bettors at a blackjack table in Vegas.

While we played poker with the children,
Each upping our ante, trying to guess at our hands.

If I make it and you don't, "Call an auctioneer."
If you make it and I don't, "Keep the books and paintings."

The eldest, just shy of 18, we all decided,
Could raise his sister.

The two banter about who gets the "master suite,"
Allowing the reason to recede.

At night we drink love. We don't pray because
We don't pray.

We peer into the abyss of each other's eyes,
And know everything is fleeting.

Even this, and we embrace again.
Again, we embrace.

The lights go out when that's all we can take.
When we are done.

Just before giving into sleep, I ask you to play
The recordings of those I loved, while I'm—

i couldn't throw you against a wall

i couldn't throw you against a wall, you
who cling to me,
crying,
asking, "how did i get here?"
and, "where are we going?"

you, whose soft roundness,
whose peapod toes hold needs
greater than mine.

i hold you close, fearful of letting go,
afraid of admitting that fierce thought to myself,
to you,
of what it says about me,
of what it says about women everywhere who
ever had a thought of letting go
that was violent.

i shove your sweet head close to my breast,
grateful for your breath.

Abandonment

Mothers leave their babies in bassinets to cry it out. Parents drop their children at schools, and slowly back away from doors and the shrieks on the other side.

The tables turn when we are asked to do drop-offs out of sight, and later when the doors are now shut on us, or we are slowly, or eagerly, pushed away.

New walls. New doors. New life.

Still later, as grandparents, we hand children back into our own children's arms: "Your turn," we say.

My children, when you pull the clothes slowly and painfully from my drawers and closets, deciding which blouses or dresses to keep, remember—

I sorted yours annually while you grew, tossing most, keeping only a few. I let you each go, one thread at a time, and managed myself not to unravel.

Abandonment is something we practice,
in order to get it right.

I know you don't want to be someone's child forever,
you just think you do.

Ordinary Sounds

Are the ones I wish to keep.

Our daughter brushing her teeth before bed. Your melodic whistling.
The way our son used to pop not his fingers but his jaw before he grew fully into it.
It was like nails on a chalkboard, but there were nails.

The knock at the door. The sliding open of the screen.
The fluffing of a pillow; the purring of the cat,
or you.

Operatic Ella Fitzgerald once hit a note so pure, Memorex made us believe
she had cracked glass.

I have trimmed the toenails of our children and their late father—there is
some solace in knowing I once could.

The sound of clipping is with me when I hear a birch fall in our woods.
I am alert: Some sounds signal danger.

So don't celebrate me with song, tell stories of the mundane:

The clinking drink delivered when you weren't sick. My cracking ankles
descending the stairs.
The creaking drawer offering the spoon before you realized you needed one.
The chewed thoughts of you when I left.

Always know that while you slept, I quietly watched.
Listen for my knocking.

At the Opera House

Do we age into the beauty of sound as we do the salted heaven of oysters and anchovies, cabernet and golden whiskeys swirling, legs viscous?

Do our mature taste buds indicate depreciation, or simply
a fully savored, beautiful acquiescence?

In the restroom during orchestra's pause, all the marble doors have been shut delicately, care offered to every liquid moment, even the ordinary now deserving of love's gestures.

Arias recalled in sweet memory, the slow trickle of urine stall by stall indicates the increasing age of those surrounding me—my own, a staccato resonance.

While I'm dying, lower my bottom jaw, and tilt my head if I no longer can.
Prop my neck with a pillow, if you must,

and squeeze the lemon, add the hot sauce, and let the oyster and me slide into darkness savoring the globulous salty sweetness of our combined lives.

A little whiskey rubbed on the lips will also do.

VIII.

A Birthday Poem for Us

My husband asks me to write for him a poem, for his birthday, and tell all that is true, in just one sentence, for him alone, but I am writing also to you because he and I knew each other before, we knew each other before, just like you and I knew each other before, before all we ever knew and will ever know, and now, in words alone, letters even more alone, these solitary letters creating words, creating communication through bravas and bravos reverberating across miles into mines and over mountains, heat waves above pavement on a blistering day in a surprise city as he rubs my forehead with his thick thumb, back and forth, back and forth, strumming the tension that is not only mine, but ours—yours too—making the music, the lovely music, that brings our breath so close the heat is all, and brings you, reader, to me, to all of us, to we, as we thrum at once, no end punctuation, no single heartbeats, all the world a single sentence, one sonic boom, one giant scroll unraveling one birthday, one deep breath-sigh for us all, with no full stop

Acknowledgments

Recognition

Best of the Net Finalist: "Outside In" (2018)
Pushcart Prize and Best of the Net nomination: "Stepping Up" (2021)
Honorable Mention in the Muskegon (Michigan) Art Museum's "Art Talks Back" contest: "Notre Amour, Comme une Pomme, Vient de la Terre" (2019)

Journals

3288 Review: "Notre Amour, Comme une Pomme, Vient de la Terre"
Anti-Heroin Chic: "River among the Gravel"
Autumn Sky Daily: "Remember This"
Amaryllis: "The kindness of strangers"
Bonnie's Crew: "The Last Time Making Love"; "Gardening is an Honor System"
Boston Literary Magazine: "The Month of the Dead"; "Phantom Limbs"
Cabinet of Heed: "The Last Unveiling"
Clementine Unbound: "At the Opera House"
Constellate Journal: "Homesick"
Corvus Review: "And then you can't breathe"
Dime Show Review: "Secret Sauce"
ELJ Editions: "Melding Metal with Metal"
Eunoia Review: "A Birthday Poem for Us"; "It's All Over Now"; "Ordinary Sounds"; "Superstitions"; "The Dancer"; "The thing is…"; "The Widow Remarries"; "To the person in charge of discontinuation:"; "Twice Believing and Twice Knowing"; "X,Y,C"
Halcyon Days: "Spring"
Ink, Sweat & Tears: "The trouble with pairs"
Melancholy Hyperbole: "Doorbell Advised"; "Most of the Days of the Week"
Muddy River Poetry Review: "Have Love"; "Night Giblets"; "The Height of Gladness"
Mused: Bella Online Literary Review: "When a leaf blowing in the wind seems like a hello"
New Verse News: "Driven Thru"
Nibble: "Upon a Poem"; "i couldn't throw you against a wall"

Nine Muses: "All the Previous Deaths were Unposted; Word Came by Ring Tone or Post, Not Post"; "Knowledge"; "Outside In"
Picaroon Poetry: "Everything I hate about you, I love about you, Dear"
Poetry Breakfast: "While your husband is still able to stand"
Poetry Quarterly: "Rose Colored Lovers"; "Times Square, 1977"
Rat's Ass Review: "In Memoriam"; "Stepping Up"; "When you reach to flush the toilet and your hand looks exactly like your mother's"
Red Eft Review: "Between Us"
The Literary Nest: "Love Begets Love"
The Opiate: "Bartering in MI"; "No One Knew"
Three Drops from a Cauldron: "Call me Charon"
Three Line Poetry: "Going Hungry"
Thimble Literary Journal: "Anointing the Dead"
Trouvaille Review: "it must be strange to be a house"
TunaFish Journal: "Abandonment"
Unbroken: "How Contentment Comes"
Yellow Chair Review: "Father's Botany Lessons"

Chapbook Reprints

Have Love (Finishing Line Press, 2019): "All the Previous Deaths were Unposted; Word Came by Ring Tone or Post, Not Post"; "Bartering in MI"; "Doorbell Advised"; "Father's Botany Lessons"; "Going Hungry"; "Have Love"; "How Contentment Comes"; "In Memoriam"; "Knowledge"; "Love Begets Love"; "No One Knew"; "Outside In"; "The Height of Gladness"; "Most of the Days of the Week"; "Phantom Limbs"; "Rose Colored Lovers"; "Superstitions"; "The Trouble with Pairs"; "While your husband is still able to stand"; "When a leaf blowing in the wind seems like a hello"; "X,Y,C"

Anthologized

The Best Emerging Poets of Michigan: "A Kiss"
The Literary Parrot Series Two: "Dish by Dish"
Through the Looking Glass: Reflecting on the Madness and Chaos Within: "When I am, play me recordings of those I loved, while I'm"
We Will Not Be Silenced: The Lived Experience of Sexual Harassment and Sexual Assault Told Powerfully through Poetry, Prose, Essay, and Art: "Sleepover"

Reprinted

Find a Place for Me: "The Last Time Making Love"
Persona Non Grata: "While your husband is still able to stand"
Vita Brevis: "Gardening is an Honor System"
Words for the Year: "Most of the Days of the Week"

Author's Note

Much gratitude to my greatest loves for always supporting me in my desire to wordsmith—my stalwart and loving husband Dave and kind and brilliant children Maeve and Liam. Thank you again to Dave, my first reader and ballast in all life things, and also to my unstinting and insightful reading team, especially poets John Cullen and Maggie Walcott. My work and I have lived better due to the smarts, wit, and support of the writers in my writing circles in Michigan and Illinois where many of these poems first saw full light. I am grateful to the editors who spurred me on by debuting many of these poems in their beautiful journals and books. Shelley Stevens, this collection would not be the same without your striking painting, "Delicious Deception," as its stunning introduction. Jennifer Johnson, your generosity and keen photographer's eye is much appreciated. I also very much appreciate the support of esteemed poet Kai Coggin, host of Wednesday Night Poetry, who generously featured a number of these poems. I am thankful for my residency time at The Writers' Colony at Dairy Hollow and the professional and financial support of the English, Literature, and World Languages Department and the College of Arts, Sciences, and Education at Ferris State University. Thank you, dear readers and supporters, all.

Dr. Deirdre Fagan is a widow, wife, mother of two, and the sole survivor of her birth family. She is the author of the award-winning memoir, *Find a Place for Me: Embracing Love and Life in the Face of Death* (2022), an award-finalist short story collection, *The Grief Eater* (2019), a chapbook of poetry, *Have Love* (2019), and a reference book, *Critical Companion to Robert Frost* (2007). Fagan is also a poetry Pushcart nominee and Best of the Net finalist. A creative writer and literary scholar whose work has recently been featured on NPR, ABC, and CBS, as well as in *Newsweek* and *HuffPost*, Fagan's poetry, fiction, and nonfiction, and critical essays on poetry, memoir, and pedagogy, have appeared widely in literary and scholarly journals, anthologies, and encyclopedias, as well as in newspapers and magazines. She holds a master's in English and a doctorate in Humanistic Studies (English and Philosophy) from University at Albany, and a bachelor's in English from University at Buffalo. Fagan is a native New Yorker who has previously lived in Arizona, Florida, Illinois, and Maryland, and currently resides in Michigan where she is a professor and the coordinator of creative writing at Ferris State University and poetry editor for *Orange Blossom Review*. Meet her at deirdrefagan.com.

www.ingramcontent.com/pod-product-compliance
Lightning Source LLC
Chambersburg PA
CBHW020335170426
43200CB00006B/395